It is likeness that begets affection.

ALEXANDER POPE, C. 1730

SEXY DOGS

SEXY
DOGS

BY J.C. SUARÈS

TEXT BY JANA MARTIN

 HarperResource
An Imprint of HarperCollins*Publishers*

To Georges,
one sexy Akita

CREATIVE DIRECTOR: J.C. Suarès
EDITOR AND PHOTO RESEARCHER: Jana Martin
DESIGNER: Hasmig M. Kacherian
All rights reserved. Printed in the United States of America. No part of this book may be used or reproduced in any manner whatsoever without written permission except in the case of brief quotations embodied in critical articles and reviews. For information address HarperCollins Publishers Inc., 10 East 53rd Street, New York, NY 10022.
HarperCollins books may be purchased for educational, business, or sales promotional use. For information please write: Special Markets Department, HarperCollins Publishers Inc., 10 East 53rd Street, New York, NY 10022.
FIRST EDITION
Library of Congress Cataloging-in-Publication Data
Suarès, Jean-Claude.
        Sexy dogs/ by Jean-Claude Suarès.
        p. cm.
ISBN 0-688-17651-8
 1. Dogs—Pictorial works. 2. Photography of dogs. 3. Dogs—Anecdotes. I. Title.
SF430 .S75 2000
636.7'0022'2—dc21
                                                    99-058361
00 01 02 03 04 QB 10 9 8 7 6 5 4 3 2 1
Thanks to the photographers and agencies for their images and stories, the animal trainers for their wisdom and anecdotes, the many dog owners for their tales and, finally, the Best Friends Animal Sanctuary in Kanab, Utah.

PAGE ONE:

HELENE TORESDOTTER

Ove, Bull Terrier, Malmö, Sweden, 1989

TITLE PAGE:

PAULETTE BRAUN

Sweet Jezebel with a Rose, Fort Lauderdale, Florida, 1994

FACING PAGE:

STUDIO PHOTOGRAPHER

Jayne Mansfield and Her Standard Poodle, Hollywood, 1950s
The star of *Will Success Spoil Rock Hunter?* and her beloved pet, in matching outfits.

INTRODUCTION

There are no fancy breeds of dogs in the wild. You won't find Standard Poodles running together in the Camargue, or packs of French Bulldogs raiding trash cans in Yellowstone National Park. And you certainly won't find any English Springer Spaniels stalking gazelles in the African bush.

Most dog breeds are in fact man-made; created, refined, and refined again, by *Homo sapiens* to conform to our own ideals of beauty. We bred dogs to be small and cuddly, like Pugs and Pomeranians; to be sleek and elegant, like Russian Wolfhounds and Salukis; to be exotic and powerful, like Anatolian Shepherds and Neapolitan

JAYNE HINDS BIDAUT
Sophie the Pug, New York City, 1998

INTRODUCTION

Mastiffs. And some dogs are more than good-looking. In fact they're downright sexy. How dogs get to be sexy, however, is a mystery.

We find Westies and Golden Retrievers wholesomely beautiful. We find Weimaraners striking, Chows practically delicious. But what of the dogs? How do they feel about each other? We know Poodles like Poodles, and Rottweilers like Rottweilers. But why does a Poodle sometimes find a Rottweiler sexy, and vice versa? Why do different breeds drool for each other?

My recent observations around the neighborhood point to a simple answer: just because. I found proof in a five-block vicinity. Who would have guessed that Kaho, a 140-pound Akita on 83rd Street and Lexington, could fall in love with Daisy, a scrawny, 30-pound mutt around the corner? Do

INTRODUCTION

her limpid terrier eyes remind him of some other unrequited canine crush? Or is it that he got tired of looking at the neighborhood's fancy purebreds? And in the park a few blocks away, there's a foreign lady whose pint-sized Chihuahua, Maximillian, mopes all day until the apple of his eye, a black Labrador named Rosie, shows up. Does he care that she's ten times his size? Not according to his owner, who swears it was love at first sight.

You can tell that Rosie is Maximillian's Marilyn Monroe, Mona Lisa, and Madonna all wrapped into one, the way he looks at her. What's more, the way she looks at him, it's clear he'll always be her Bogart, her Connery, her Cruise. Even when she's gotten fat and his muzzle has turned gray, it's clear that they're in it to the end.

— J.C. Suarès

My mom says that Zasu, our Greyhound, is the Audrey Hepburn of dogs. You should see her in a black turtleneck. She was born with natural eyeliner, a perfect figure, and the ability to strike a pose. No wonder she was a failure at the racetrack. Clearly, she's got other things on her mind.

HILLARY JACKSON, PROFESSIONAL DOGWALKER

PRECEDING PAGES:

LARS PETER ROOS
Shall We Go for a Jaunt? Oland, Sweden, 1995

JIM DRATFIELD/PAUL COUGHLIN
Garbo Dog, New York City, 1994
"Franny, an older mixed breed, was a little reclusive, which made me think of Greta Garbo. That's why I put the scarf on."

If my Huskies, Hank and June, get into a fight, it lasts only a minute. Then they always kiss and make up. I often wonder if their sole purpose of fighting is to be able to make up. Ever watch two hundred-pound dogs hug each other?

ANDY SARBOZA, METALSMITH

PRECEDING PAGES, LEFT:
CRIS KELLY
Shiba Inu, Napa Valley, California, 1999

PRECEDING PAGES, RIGHT:
AMERICAN IMAGES INCORPORATED
Young Female Border Collie in Our Studio, New York City, 1997

DENNIS STOCK
Siberian Husky on a Chevrolet Truck, Skagway, Alaska, 1999

PHOTOGRAPHER UNKNOWN

Ava Gardner and German Shepherd, Hollywood, late 1940s

KERRY HAYES

Nicole Kidman and Pomeranian in *To Die For*, 1995

JANA DE PEYER
Laura Dern and Pal at the Best Friends Animal Sanctuary, Kanab, Utah, 1999

STUDIO PHOTOGRAPHER
Sandra Dee and Friends, Hollywood, 1959
The star of *Gidget* poses by the pool with her French Poodle and Pomeranian.

Then Ball, my cut-tailed cur,
  and I begin to play.
He o'er my sheep-hook leaps,
  now th'one, now th'other way,
Then on his hinder feet
  he doth himself advance,
I tune, and to my note
  my lively dog will dance.

MICHAEL DRAYTON
"DANCING DOG"

BRUNO BARBEY
Chez Balthus, Rossinière, Switzerland, 1995
Setsuko, wife of the painter Balthus (Count Balthasar Klossowki),
at the piano with daughter Haruni and the family Dalmation.

I picked Salukis as Best-in-Show because frankly
I've never seen sexier creatures.

JUDGE, AMERICAN KENNEL CLUB

JIM DRATFIELD/JOANNE GIGANTI
Salukis Swooning, New York City, 1996
"These two live together. They're sexy dogs.
Mysterious, enigmatic, and even more elegant than the
chair. You can tell they turn each other on.
They're whispering sweet nothings to each other."

PRECEDING PAGES:

RICHARD KALVAR

Two Dogs with a Frisbee, Washington, D.C., 1999

PHOTOGRAPHER UNKNOWN

The Stars of *101 Dalmatians*, Hollywood, 1996

AMERICAN IMAGES INCORPORATED

Dachshund Pair in Our Studio, New York City, 1997

Sexiest Dog Breeds by Dog Run, Random Survey,
New York City:

    Tompkins Square Park: Pit Bull

    Washington Square Park: Rhodesian Ridgeback

    Madison Square Park: Standard Poodle

    Carl Shurz Park: Dachshund

    Riverside Park: Mutt

SUMMER 1999

ELLIOTT ERWITT
Two Dogs, Capri, Italy, 1977

I have several dogs in my make-up. I fight a bit.
The spaniel part of me gets excited at the sound of gun-fire,
But then my memory of being a poodle
Evokes a bloody wing, the eye of a dying hind,
I remember what a rabbit puts into its last look
And I feel stirring within me my heart of a Saint Bernard.

EDMOND ROSTAND

PATOU

KARL BADEN
S.A.F. and Badger, Syracuse, New York, 1976
"This was taken on a spring day, when we were all taking a break from classes to soak up the sunshine. Badger was my dog, a pure Siberian Husky."

"Lovey"
is something
of a
nomenclatural
tin can
on the
tail
of one's
self-respect.

O. HENRY

"MEMOIRS OF A YELLOW DOG"

SEXY

34

DOGS

DANTE BURN-FORTI
The Fastest Dog in the World, County Cork, Ireland, c. 1996

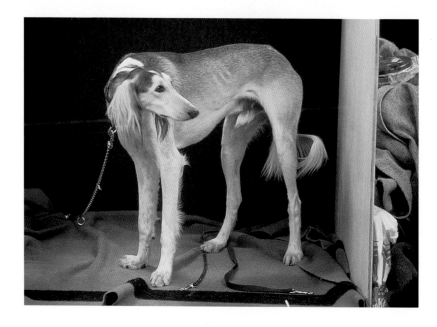

ELLIOTT ERWITT
Saluki at the Dog Show, New York City, 1980

DR. AND MRS. J. DARRELL BLACK
Ch. Sundown Alabaster Treasure, San Andreas, California, 1996
"In the game of conquest that love really is, Salukis are champions.
You can catch them only by turning and running like hell. You have
to make them chase you."

LeRoy describes a dog, whose great-grandfather was a wolf, and this dog showed a trace of its wild parentage only in one way, by not coming in a straight line to his master when called.

CHARLES DARWIN

ON THE ORIGINS OF SPECIES BY MEANS OF NATURAL SELECTION

SEXY

DOGS

G. PINKHASSOV
Bonney Brig, River Thames, England, 1994

Star's a diva. When it's time to go home from the park, she delays us by flirting with her admirers.

GAYE BOWIDAS, PROFESSIONAL

BALLROOM DANCER

HELENE TORESDOTTER
Kameo, Chinese Crested Dog, Malmö, Sweden, 1989

This is my dog story, starring my mother's Pomeranian, in which a toy dog that weighs about ten pounds barks as loud as a German Shepherd and heads into turf battles like Napoleon.

BETSEY FARGAS, PROFESSIONAL DOG TRAINER

RON KRISEL
Pomeranian, Los Angeles, 1994

"Well, well, Vixen, you foolish wench, what is it, what is it? I must go in, must I? Ay, ay, I'm never to have a will o' my own anymore. And those pups, what do you think I'm to do with 'em, when they're twice as big as you—for I'm pretty sure the father was that hulking Bull-terrier of Will Baker's—wasn't he now, eh, you sly hussy?" (Here Vixen tucked her tail between her legs, and ran forward into the house. Subjects are sometimes broached which a well-bred female will ignore.)

GEORGE ELIOT

ADAM BEDE

ELLIOTT ERWITT
New York City, 1980
A Standard Poodle awaits her turn in the ring at the Westminster Kennel Club dog show.

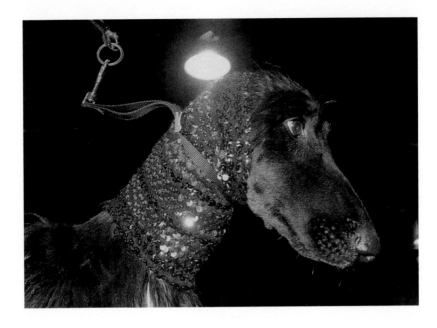

KARL BADEN
Boston, Massachusetts, 1993
"This was at a dog show. I love the Afghan Hound's headwrap and jewelry."

ELLIOTT ERWITT
Great Dane at the Dog Show, New York City, 1980

Why do you think they call it "puppy dog eyes"? Doesn't matter whether it's James Dean or a Golden Retriever. When they fix you with that look, you're helpless. Whatever they want, they get.

<u>WIBKE REIMANN,</u> FASHION PHOTOGRAPHER

BLAKE LITTLE
Best Friends, Malibu, California, 1998
Four-time Olympic gold medalist diver Greg Louganis with his Great Dane, Freeway.

All animals except man know that the ultimate aim of life is to enjoy it.

SAMUEL BUTLER

STUDIO PHOTOGRAPHER
Yvette Mimieux, Hollywood, California, 1960s
The movie star relaxes at home with her pets, a brindle Great Dane and a tame leopard.

I'm fond of telling people that dogs know what women have forgotten: let men think they're in charge, always play hard to get, and bark at anyone who gets too fresh.

KAREN BLACK, SALUKI BREEDER

STUDIO PHOTOGRAPHER
Jayne Mansfield with Her Dogs, Hollywood, 1950s
The platinum-haired pinup and movie star with her dogs, a Scottish Terrier and a Standard Poodle.

They talk sweet girlish prattle
to this animal (when there is
anyone near enough to
overhear them), and they
kiss its nose, and put its unwashed
head up against their cheek in
a most touching manner;
though I have noticed that
these caresses are principally
performed when there are
young men hanging about.

JEROME K. JEROME

IDLE THOUGHTS FOR AN IDLE FELLOW

JOHN ENGSTEAD
Ava Gardner, Hollywood, late 1940s
The future star of *The Barefoot Contessa* poses with her
Dalmatian in the California sunshine.

My terrier, Doreen, gets her way on a limited but effective repertoire:

1. In pet stores, she embarrasses me into buying treats by barking.

2. In public, she prevents me from scolding her in front of strangers by sitting up and begging.

3. On walks, she tricks me into stopping so she can meet handsome young dogs by pretending to need to pee every block.

4. At home, she guilts me into letting her sleep on the bed by just being there.

D. DONAHUE, JOURNALIST

PRECEDING PAGES:

THOMAS HOEPKER
Washington Square Park, New York City, 1983

AMERICAN IMAGES INCORPORATED
Jack Russell Listening, New York City, 1997

O 'tis a foul thing
when a cur cannot
keep himself
in all companies.
I would have,
as one should say,
one that takes upon him
to be a dog indeed,
to be,
as it were,
a dog at all things.

WILLIAM SHAKESPEARE

THE TWO GENTLEMEN OF VERONA

KARL BADEN
New York City, 1999
"I saw this woman in SoHo and asked if I could take a picture
of her dog. Sometimes they say yes, sometimes they say no. But
it's always important to ask."

KARL BADEN
Boston, Massachusetts, 1993
"I find the getups on the dogs backstage even more interesting than what they wear in the show ring."

KARL BADEN
Boston, Massachusetts, 1993
"I usually shoot first and ask questions later. At the Bay Colony Dog Show, a rumor went around that I was a PETA spy and they threw me out. I had to eat a lot of crow to be let back in."

Let me tell you it's not this old salt the ladies go for. If I meet a girl on the beach, she's interested in my dog Pete, not me. Pete's a water dog: if he were human he'd be a blond-haired surfer. Lucky for me he's just a Labrador Retriever.

FRANK LUCCIA, TOURBOAT CAPTAIN

ROLF NYSTRÖM
Deep Blue Sea, Sweden, c. 1990

STEVE MCCURRY

Producer David Wolper and Poodle on the Walk of Fame,
Hollywood, 1995

ELLIOTT ERWITT
Photograph Taken for a Shoe Advertisement with Lhasa Apso
and Weimaraner, New York City, 1989

He swam to land with a lily in his mouth, which he came and laid at my foot.

WILLIAM COWPER

PRECEDING PAGES:

COSTA MANOS
Resting on the Patio, Greece, 1963

BURT GLINN
At the Beach, 1961

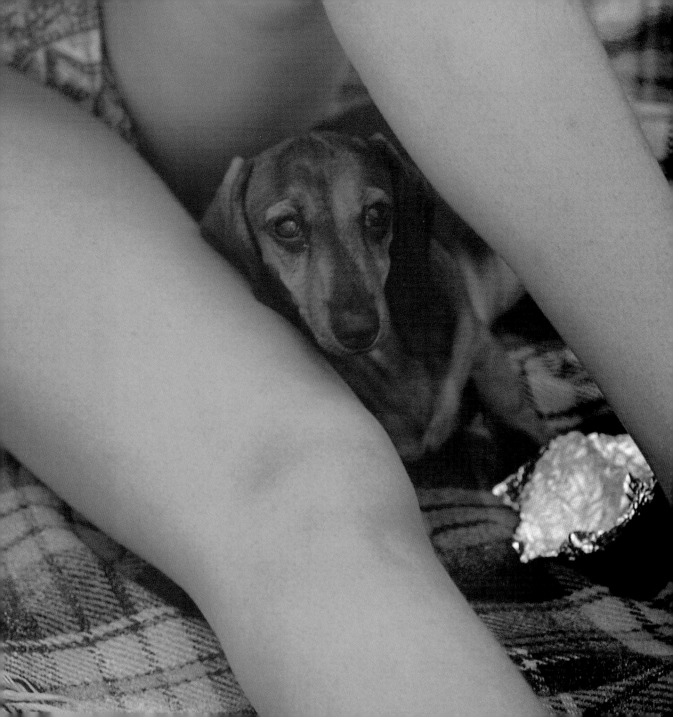

ELLIOTT ERWITT
Bulldog and Leg, New York City, 1989

ERNST HAAS

John Cusack, Meredith Salenger, and the Wolf from
Journey of Natty Gann, 1985

STUDIO PHOTOGRAPHER

Joe Lando and Chaz the Malamute from *Dr. Quinn, Medicine Woman*, 1995

MONTY BRINTON

Paul Gross and Diefenbaker the Siberian Husky, Costars of *Due South*, Ontario, 1996

HARRY HAMBURG
Bill Clinton and Buddy, the First Dog,
Washington, D.C., 1998

PHOTOGRAPHER UNKNOWN
Kirk Douglas and Friend, Hollywood, 1950s

Photo Credits

© American Images Incorporated/FPG LLC, pp. 15, 29, 59
© Karl Baden, pp. 33, 46, 61, 62, 63
© Bruno Barbey/Magnum Photos, p. 23
© Jayne Hinds Bidaut, p. 6
© Dr. and Mrs. J. Darrell Black, p. 37
© Paulette Braun, title page, back cover
Monty Brinton, © Archive Newsphotos, p. 77
© Dante Burn-Forti/Tony Stone Images, p. 35
© CBS/Photofest, p. 76
© Columbia Pictures, Inc., courtesy The Kobal Collection, p. 19
© Jana de Peyer for Best Friends Animal Sanctuary, Kanab, Utah, p. 20
© Walt Disney Productions/Photofest, p. 28
© Jim Dratfield's Petography, Inc., pp. 13, 25
© John Engstead, courtesy The Kobal Collection, p. 55
© Elliott Erwitt/Magnum Photos, pp. 31, 36, 45, 47, 67, 73
© FPG LLC, p. 21
© Burt Glinn/Magnum Photos, p. 71
© Henry Gris/FPG LLC, pp. 51, 79
© Ernst Haas/Photofest, pp. 74–75
© Thomas Hoepker/Magnum Photos, pp. 56–57
© Richard Kalvar/Magnum Photos, pp. 26–27
© Cris Kelly, p. 14
Courtesy The Kobal Collection, pp. 5, 18, 53
© Ron Krisel/Tony Stone Images, p. 43
© Blake Little, p. 49
© Steve McCurry/Magnum Photos, p. 66
© Costa Manos/Magnum Photos, pp. 68–69
© Rolf Nyström/Tiofoto, p. 65
© G. Pinkhassov/Magnum Photos, pp. 38–39
© Priscilla Rattazzi, p. 4
© Dennis Stock/Magnum Photos, p. 17
© Lars Peter Roos/Tiofoto, front cover, pp. 10–11
© Helene Toresdotter/Tiofoto, p. 1, 41
Harry Hamburg, courtesy The White House, p. 78